Praise for *When the Night Agrees to Speak to Me*

If I had only one word to define Ananda Devi's *When the Night Agrees to Speak to Me,* it would be aliveness—a synonym, plausibly, in Devi's idiolect, for freedom. Everything—from the Night in the title, to skin, to mud, to a green sari, to sound, to Time itself—is alive. And everything is body. Furiously, magnificently, body, bodied, bodies pulsating with a hard-won freedom that perhaps requires words, poetry, as lifeblood, for "Poetry is our vein a door without it words die a slow death." Translated with confident, calm dexterity and breathtaking attention by Kazim Ali, this is a collection that held my body—eyes and heart and brain—in its jaws from beginning till end.   **—Karthika Naïr**

Ananda Devi is an Indian writer from Mauritius now living in France, or a French writer with her roots on the island and South Asia, or a Mauritian writer in the tradition of great colonized voices who have renewed French poetry and prose—or a feminist poet and novelist without borders. This book of harsh lyric and enigmatic, theoretical and erotic prose, takes on a second life in Kazim Ali's sensitive translation.   **—Marilyn Hacker**

The work of Mauritian poet Ananda Devi is rightly celebrated in the Francophone world and in *When the Night Agrees to Speak to Me*, the Anglophone world gets a glimpse of the depth and complexity of this writer's thinking and lived experience. In Kazim Ali's translation, the allusive density of Ananda Devi's poetry is clarified and given air. We see the way Devi transfers agency to the real and the abstract: the 'mud about which / The future has nothing to say' and also the 'woman erased by her bruises'. Devi's poetry has suffering, resignation but also a deep, visceral joy that shines through. Ali, as a poet himself, is very conscious of what it takes to live upon an earth riven by borders and crossings of all kinds, and he brings all of that experience to this translation.   **—Sridala Swan**

When the Night Agrees to Speak to Me

Ananda Devi

TRANSLATED FROM
THE FRENCH BY KAZIM ALI

PHONEME
MEDIA

DEEP
VELLUM

DALLAS, TEXAS

Phoneme Media, an imprint of Deep Vellum
3000 Commerce St., Dallas, Texas 75226
deepvellum.org · @deepvellum

Deep Vellum Publishing
3000 Commerce St., Dallas, Texas 75226
deepvellum.org · @deepvellum

Deep Vellum is a 501c3 nonprofit literary arts organization
founded in 2013 with the mission to bring
the world into conversation through literature.

Translation first published in India in 2021 by Harper Perennial
An Imprint of HarperCollins *Publishers*
A-75, Sector 57, Noida, Uttar Pradesh 201301, India
Originally published in 2011 as *Quand la nuit consent à me parler*
by Éditions Bruno Doucey, Paris

ISBN: 978-1-64605-188-5 (paperback)
ISBN: 978-1-64605-189-2 (eBook)

LIBRARY OF CONGRESS CONTROL NUMBER: 2022932166

Exterior design by Daniel Benneworth-Gray
Text set in 11/15 Arno Pro

PRINTED IN THE UNITED STATES OF AMERICA

Contents

Quand la nuit consent à me parler

When the Night Agrees to Speak to Me

1

À l'aube, tu descendras pieds nus
Boire à la rivière
Comme ces chats muets
Aux pattes cramoisies

Tu glisseras sur les pentes
Endormies de plaisir
Suivre la piste argentée
Des limaces écrasées

Tu iras au midi chercher l'évidence
Qu'un jour ici tu as vécu
Qu'il y avait des enfants, des amis,
Un amour, une constance

De tout cela ne demeure
Que le ciel bas, les herbes grasses,
L'eau violente,
Les ruches abandonnées

Tu tends l'oreille
Aux voix des absents
Jusqu'à ce que la nuit enfin
Consente à te parler.

1

At dawn you will descend barefoot
Like a silent cat
On crimson paws
To drink from the river

You'll slip down the bank
Foggy with pleasure
In the silver tracks
Of trampled snails

To the south you will search
For some proof you lived here once
Had children, friends,
A love that lasted

But nothing's left of all that
Just the low sky, the river grasses,
Wild water,
Abandoned beehives

Your ears strain to hear
The voices of those absent
Until the night at last
Agrees to speak to you.

2

Je ne vous connais pas
J'ignore jusqu'à votre nom
Votre visage m'est étrange
Balafré de sa rage

Quand vous déchirerez ma page
Vous saurez qui j'étais
Un trou, un remous
Un déchet sur un rêve

Vous le maître de nos destins
Dont je ne connais pas le nom
D'où vous vient cette colère
Cette fureur sans pardon ?

J'ai eu beau fuir
Vous me ramenez
Me tirant par les cheveux
Comme la dernière des damnées.

2

I don't know you
Am unaware of your name
Your face unfamiliar
Scarred by its rage

When you tear up my page
You will know who I was
A wound, an upheaval,
A scrap from a dream

You, the master of our fate
Whose name I do not know
From where comes all this anger
This unforgiving fury?

I fled fast as I could
But you brought me back
Dragging me by the hair
Like the last of the damned.

3

Que cette pluie soit la dernière
Le dernier mot de la prière
Avant que les lèvres s'éteignent
Dans la bouche du vent

Que cette marche solitaire
Dans le sillon de vos pas
Ne revienne plus en arrière
Chercher les ailes percées

Que ma main obtempérée
Ne s'allie plus à une autre main
Pour se refermer sur l'air
De tous ces corps abandonnés

Que mon demain soit un hier
Puisque rien n'est plus à faire
À construire ni à détruire
Rien est déjà là : jamais.

3

That this rain should be the last
The last word of my prayer
Before my lips are sealed shut
By the mouth of the wind

That this lonely walk
In your footsteps
Should never circle back
To search for the pierced wings

That my hand, once compliant
Should not join another's
To close upon the void
Of abandoned bodies

That my tomorrow be a yesterday
Since nothing is left to accomplish
Nothing to build or to destroy
Nothing has already become: Never.

4

Ferme la porte, clos ton destin
Efface du miroir
Le glacier de tes yeux

Tremble à genoux
Sur le seuil dérobé
Des vertus impossibles

Ne jamais être femme
Si le corps écartelé
Ne peut plus vous offrir

Sa glaire empoisonnée
Ni la soierie fine
Si finement déchirée

Si richement démembrée
Par l'assaut des couleurs
Quand le noir n'a plus lieu

Tissu de mes mensonges
Du rire dissimulé
Derrière mes lèvres fermées

Si je ne m'éveille
Repue de tous mes rêves
Festives écorchures.

4

Close the door, shut down your fate
Wipe from that mirror
The ice of your eyes

Tremble on your knees
At the secret threshold
Of impossible virtue

Never to be a woman
If a body split asunder
Cannot offer you any more

Neither its poisonous fluids
Nor its exquisite silks
So finely shredded
So richly dismembered
By the assault of colour
When the darkness is no longer

Fabric of my lies
Of laughter hidden
behind my sealed lips

Filled if I don't rouse myself
With all my dreams,
Those festive flayings.

5

Dehors les ronces attendent
La nourriture de leurs plaies

Nos yeux errent sanglants
Dans leurs noires harmonies

L'eau sur ma peau
Est une robe d'acide.

5

Outside, the brambles wait
To be fed by wounds

Our eyes wander bloody
In their dark harmonies

Rain on my skin
A gown of acid.

6

Il a pris un couteau pour s'entailler les mains
Dans ses yeux une lueur de crucifié
Dans son corps une guerre d'avance perdue
Dans son coeur la certitude
De n'être jamais né.

6

He took a knife to slice his hands
In his eyes the gleam of one crucified
In his body a war long since lost
In his heart the certainty
of never having been born.

7

Et pourquoi t'empêcherais-je de fuir
Quand le limon se dessèche
Que le goémon envahit le seuil
De l'odeur fade de la mer

Quand le sable est si noir
Que le vent sur la langue
A un goût de noyade
Et que le sel te troue la peau

Que la vérité sorte de ces corps
Fracturés sur leurs récifs
Le limon entre dans leur bouche
La grève s'éloigne des galets

Fuient rêves et mémoires
Visages immergés
Ne restera de l'île
Que les pas des absents.

7

And why would I keep you from leaving
When the silt has hardened
When seaweed crossed the threshold
Carrying with it the faint smell of the sea

When the sand is so black
That the wind on your tongue
Tastes of drowning
And the salt pierces your skin

Let the truth leave these bodies
Shipwrecked on their reefs
Silt in their mouths
Shore stretching away from the wrack-line rubble

Dreams and memories fleeing
Submerged faces
And of the island there only remains
Footsteps echoing of those long since gone.

8

Je ne vivrai pas plus que de besoin
C'est ce qu'a dit ma mère
C'est ce qu'a dit mon père

Il faut savoir partir quand il est encore temps.

8

I will not live more than I need
This is what my mother said
This is what my father said

You have to know to leave when there is still time.

9

Enlève ma peau. Dévêts-moi de moi.
Regarde de plus près :
Lis ma fortune dans mes entrailles.

Les racines sur ma main
Disent déjà tout
Avant même que de naître.

Tu ne m'as pas crue
Quand je t'ai montré ma mort
Dans la cadence de mes chevilles.

Il suffisait pourtant d'entendre
L'effraie dans l'arbre
Qui criait au moment précis de nos amours.

9

Peel back my skin. Unclothe me of myself.
Look closer:
Read a fortune in my guts.

The root-lines in my palm
Say everything already
Even about the time before my birth.

You didn't believe me
When I showed you my death
In the cadence of my step.

Yet it was enough to hear
The owl in the tree
Crying out in time with our love.

10

Il dit
Je suis né sans savoir
Sans miroir pour me dire

Qui est cet autre qui me regarde
Comme si je n'existais pas
Celui qui a semé en moi

Tant de doutes tant de folie
Tant de combats tant de colère
Tant de murs tant d'innocence

C'est moi, dit-il,
Ce n'est rien que moi.

10

He says
I was born without knowing
No mirror to tell me

Who is that other one who looks at me
Like I don't exist

The one who sowed in me
So many doubts so much craziness
So much struggle so much anger
So many barricades so much innocence

It's me, he says,
It's just me.

11

Danse avec le diable qui seul
Sait rire et seul sait souffrir
Rien d'autre ne compte
Danse avec le diable
Qui t'offre le monde
Dans un grain de sable
Et l'infini dans la chair des dieux.

11

Dance with the devil who alone
Knows laughter and alone suffering
Nothing else matters
Dance with the devil
Who offers you the world
In a grain of sand
And infinity in the flesh of gods.

12

Il m'est venu l'envie
Des dragées fines et blanches
Qui un jour épellent l'oubli
De l'autre domaine du silence

Vous me nourrirez, vous,
Mes époux de quelques jours,
Quand je n'aurai plus la force
De me nourrir seule

Certains gestes semblent si simples
Qui abolissent la vie
Refermez bien fort
Votre poing sur mon corps.

12

There came to me the desire
For pills delicate and white
That one day spell out oblivion
From the other kingdom of silence

You will feed me, you,
My sometimes spouses,
When I no longer have the strength
To feed myself

Certain gestures seem so simple
They abolish life
Firmly clench again
Your fist on my body.

13

Ce que j'ai oublié :
le goût du vent et la mollesse
d'autres lèvres. J'essaie de m'en souvenir,
l'odeur de la terre
par temps d'après la pluie,
le toucher d'un autre corps
par temps d'après l'amour

La somme des instants n'aboutit à rien
Inutile survie—la mort est très surfaite
Il n'y avait rien avant et rien non plus après.

La nuit ne t'en veut pas d'être :
C'est le jour qui se venge de toi.

13

What I forgot:
The taste of wind and the softness
Of another's lips. I try to remember
The smell of earth
After rain
The touch of another's body
After love

The sum of moments comes to nothing
Survival feels useless: death is so overrated
There was nothing before and will be nothing after.

Night claims to have no business with you:
It is the day that aims to exact its revenge.

14

Lui, l'énergumène des jours
Celui qui sifflote fort quand tous les autres se taisent
Gai quand il eût fallu être triste
Muet quand on veut l'écouter ·
Mais qui chante en parcourant tes lieux
son fief son éternité
Même quand il trahit enchante
Même quand il disparaît
Te hante

Bel énergumène.

14

He's the odd one out
Who whistles loudly when everyone else is silent
Happy when one ought to have been sad
Mute when one wants to listen
But sings running past you
His realm his eternity
Even when he betrays, he delights
Even when he disappears
He haunts you

Moon-wild beauty.

15

L'oeil se grée de rire pour mieux taire
Les larmes des enfants solitaires
Qui laissent sur leur coeur de verre
Des striures pastel.

15

Laughter rigs the eye better to hide
Tears of lonely children
That leave pastel streaks
On glass hearts.

16

Tu me boiras en retour de peine
Toi qui fus quand je n'étais que friche
Tu brûleras tes ailes à me sillonner
Sans joie
Comme on massacre une baleine.
Le silence est une aube de granit
Sursaut des sens lorsque crisse la nuit.

16

You will drink of me for all your trouble
You who existed when I was still fallow
You will burn up your wings ploughing furrows into me
Without joy
As one harpoons a whale.
Silence is a granite dawn
Surge of senses as the night grinds groaning past.

17

Frémis ta chair à la recherche d'un nom
Fouille dans tes interstices
La tempête douce à tes yeux
A un vieux goût de refrain oublié.

17

Thrill your flesh searching for a name
Frisk all your crevices
The storm, sweet to your eyes,
Has lingering notes of some forgotten tune.

18

Tu es la portée du silence
Et le bruit par lequel il se rompt
La parole est l'ultime reniement
Il n'y eût de meurtres sans mots pour les dire
Que peux-tu bien avoir à dire ?
Parole imparfaite, parole défaite.

18

You are the measure of silence
And the noise that breaks it
The word is final denial
There were no murders without words to name them
What is left for you to say?
Imperfect word, word defeated.

19

Décharge d'impossible
Brûlure de mains à pleine pierre
À dire vrai je me préfère sorcière
Damnée d'éternité
La bouche flétrie de mots
Qu'allonger ma vie au service de l'ennui
Pas de choix que de mentir à soi-même—
Ainsi faisait Narcisse face à son image.

19

Static shock of the impossible
Hands burned on bare stone
To tell the truth I prefer witchcraft
Cursed with eternity
Mouth branded with words
To the lengthening of my life in service of tedium
No choice but to lie to oneself—
like Narcissus face to face with his image.

20

Trop d'absence
Ainsi sommes-nous parties
Lèvres longtemps tachées
Du jus des muselières

Graver dans nos vieilles mains
L'ombre poudreuse de nos voiles
Assouplir nos yeux
Grevés de trop de ciel

Tant de bruit ne peut
Que taire la lumière

Ainsi pliées nous voyageons
Sur nos orteils brisés
Femmes de sable le vent nous efface
Nous ne danserons plus sur les ronces.

20

Too much absence
And so we left
Our lips long stained
By the sweat of our muzzles

Engraving on our aged hands
The powdery snow of our veils
Softening our eyes
Struck by too many skies

So much noise cannot
But silence the light

So bent we walk
On our broken toes
Women of sand, the wind erases us
We will dance no more upon thorns.

21

Quand ne restera plus de nos mémoires
Que les chemins des marées
Et la moisson du soleil

Vous partirez en nombre profilées de vous-mêmes
Sans lutte et sans sourire pour avoir trop vécu
Dépossédées de vos douleurs et de vos rires
Déployées de vos vertus et de vos faix

N'ayant pour tout miroir que l'immobile présent
Acceptant la nuit de vos cuisses épandues
Vos riches humeurs votre moquerie du bonheur
Votre mépris de l'envie
Semant des gouttes de vous-mêmes
Sang liquide amniotique pertes blanches
Tout ce qui fait de vous des femmes
Mais est-ce tout, n'est-ce que cela que faites-vous
Du reste puits crevasse trou d'inexploré
De rage magnétique de puissance maléfique

Vous tendez le doigt et le monde se plie
Vous tendez les yeux et la vie s'agenouille

Mais l'égal partage vous est interdit.

21

When nothing remains of our memories
But the path of the tides
And the harvest of sunlight

In numbers you will leave shadowed by yourselves
Without struggle or a smile for having lived so much
Dispossessed of your sorrows and laughter
Your virtues and burdens unfurling

Your only mirror the unmoving present
Your thighs spreading to accept the night
Your rich fluids your mockery of happiness
Your scorn of envy
Seeding drops of yourselves
Blood amniotic fluid slickness from your core
All that's made you women
But is that all, is there nothing else what about
The rest a well a crevasse an unexplored reach
Of magnetic rage of malicious power

You point your finger and the world bends
You focus your gaze and life itself kneels

But an equal stake you are denied.

22

Les verrous sont éclatés
La porte est ouverte
À jamais impossible
Le premier pas hors de moi.

22

The bolts are broken
The door swings open
Forever impossible
That first step outside of myself.

23

Qu'as-tu dit hier et que diras-tu
Demain
Qui n'a été dit aujourd'hui ?
Ta présence mime un secret
Depuis bien longtemps révélé.

23

What did you say yesterday and
What will you say
Tomorrow
That wasn't said today?
Your presence apes a secret
That has long been told.

24

Tu ne gardes de ma présence
Que de belles courbes déformées
Femme je ne serai jamais
Que le vain nom de l'indécence.

24

Of my presence, you remember nothing
But these beautiful distorted curves
The woman I will never be
Except in vain indecent name.

25

Quand la nuit consent à me parler
C'est à la lame
Qu'elle émince
Les lieux de certitude
Qu'elle mutile
Les aimés en solitude

Quand la nuit consent à me parler
C'est pour me dire
Les mots qui n'ont pas su
Inciser dans mes mains
L'infamie longtemps tue
Belles racines de folie

Quand la nuit consent à me parler
C'est me tournant le dos
Parce que nul arbre ne pousse
Sur le lisse de ma peau
Je n'ai pas bien souffert
Ni bien ri ni bien aimé
Le peu ne la contente pas
Ni amie ni ennemie
Elle voudrait que je danse.

25

When the night agrees to speak to me
It is with a blade
That slices
Into the places of certainty
That carves
Love into loneliness

When the night agrees to speak to me
It is to tell me
The words that didn't know
How to cut into my hands
An infamy long unsaid
Sweet lines of madness

When the night agrees to speak to me
It is with its back turned
Because neither tree nor sapling
Grows from my smooth skin
I haven't suffered enough
Nor laughed well nor loved enough
It will not be content with just a little
Neither lover nor enemy
It wants me to dance.

À présent couchée
Sur les branches du manguier
À peine un remous
Sur le verre du ciel
Elle retrousse ses plis
Pour ne pas se salir
Je ne suis que boue
Inconnue du futur.

As I lie now in the branches
Of the mango tree
Barely a whirl or eddy
In the glass of the sky
It holds back its hem
From my soiled remains
I am nothing but mud
About which the future has nothing to say.

26

Tu ne sais pas vieillir.
Tes trous intérieurs
créent des courants d'air
Tu crois te reconnaître
Mais tout ne sera que vide

L'écriture n'aura jamais été
Que le plus bref des mystères.

26

You don't know how to age
Your wounds have opened you
To all the winds
You think you know yourself
But all you will have is emptiness

Writing will have been nothing
But the briefest of mysteries.

27

Il n'y a plus rien
Là où n'était qu'un corps.

Je ne te vois plus
Là-bas éparpillée

Honte
De ne pas bien savoir mourir.

27

There is nothing left
Where once was a body.

I don't see you any more
Scattered there

Shame
Of never really knowing how to die.

28

Conseils ?
De la nuit ne demeure
Que le mépris des draps
Et au sol
Un roulis de saris verts
Indifférents au sort
De la femme annulée
Masquée par ses bleus.

28

Advice?
Night left nothing
But scorn for the bedsheets
And on the floor
An unrolled swathe of green sari
Indifferent to the lot
Of a woman erased
By her bruises.

29

D'avoir été trop mâchée
L'ombre a un goût de bagasse
Dont ne s'effacera ni le chancre ni la crasse

Je n'en parle que pour l'impression
D'avoir un peu existé

Je n'en parle que parce que les mots
Peuvent malgré moi
Remplacer la foi

Je n'en parle que parce que la fatigue du temps
Dans mes yeux est une poussière
Qui abolit toute brilliance

Et nous vivons de l'invisible
Libres mais estropiés estropiés mais libres.

29

Having been chewed too much
The darkness has the dry taste of already juiced sugarcane
Riddled with canker and dross

I only speak of it
To believe I've lived a little

I only speak of it
Because the words are able,
In spite of me, to replace faith

I only speak of it
Because the weariness of time is like dust in my eyes
That tarnishes any glow

And we live in the invisible
Free but crippled, crippled but free.

30

Cette chose gluante
Issue du corps
Annonçant chaque mois
Sa pure fatalité
J'ai désappris à vivre
Jusqu'à ce qu'il ne reste plus grand-chose
De cette purée de poix.

30

This sticky thing
Issuing from my body
Announcing every month
Its fatal purity
I forgot what it was to live
Until there were no more grand entrances
Of this resinous muck.

Les mots meurent de mort lente

Envie de poésie parce que sans elle les mots meurent de mort lente les mots égarent les sens ensevelis et les tournures troubles d'une langue explorant des pays carmin sans elle la langue ne reçoit que l'éjaculat du mépris la bouche s'ouvre sur un jus tiède et fade déversé par ondes interposées et nous pauvres complices subjugués par ces mastications inutiles ces épanchements paroxystiques d'un ventre mou nous pauvres conjurés d'un jour d'une heure gaspillant notre voix et nos convictions sans autre consolation parce que ainsi persuadés pauvres convaincus

vaincus d'avance par l'absence de mots vrais de mots qui font ce que les mots doivent faire c'est-à-dire semer le doute et récolter la déraison cingler les passions et longer les frissons plier l'infini en quatre et griffer l'obscurité des ongles tout cela oui oui mais sans poésie les mots dérapent dérivent détraquent les mots érigent des murs de mensonges et le hasard glacé d'une honte sans poésie vous n'auriez sous les doigts que le squelette du silence une peau momifiée qui ne recouvre ni chair ni sensualité des orbites vides de tout regard des lèvres retroussées sur l'inutile

la poésie est notre veine porte sans elle les mots meurent de mort lente

Words Die a Slow Death

Reaching for poetry because without it words die a slow death words that lose the sense unsensed the troubled turns of tongue exploring carmine countries without it language receives only spurts of scorn the mouth opens to warm and tasteless liquid poured out by lapping waves and we poor accomplices subjugated by this useless chewing this gasping outpouring of a soft belly we poor conspirators of one day one hour squandering our voices our votes our convictions without any consolation because we are so convinced poor convicted

Beaten already by the absence of true words words that do what words are supposed to do that is to say sowing doubt and harvesting nonsense whipping up passions and extending the thrill folding infinity in quarters and scratching at the surface all this yes yes but without poetry words skid drift break down words erect walls of lies and icy danger of shame without poetry you would have under your fingers only the skeleton of silence a mummified skin that could have neither flesh nor sensuality every glance an empty orbit lips furled around uselessness

Poetry is our vein a door without it words die a slow death

Poétique des îles

J'aurais pu écrire poétiquement les îles puisque se trace au gré de leurs constellations notre destin sur l'océan; parler du fond de cette résonance, du lapement de l'eau sur les sens et oublier que leur sol volcanique et leurs racines basaltiques sont le seul ancrage qui les empêche de dérader, qu'elles portent en elles le piétinement du temps, de l'époque, des hommes amenuisés que nous sommes devenus.

Et puis non.

Je n'en ai que faire de la poétique des îles. Des infusions de verdure en homéopathie sublimée, du bleu fallacieux de nos ciels, de nos appeaux à la fluette et maigrelette musique—sinistres pâtres— de nos appâts en attente comme des filles à la bouche infiniment ouverte

j'en ai marre de mordre et de manger cette poussière-là, de la gratter de mes pattes grêles à la recherche de pépites littéraires

rien à faire rien à foutre des images désarrimées de nos terres

reflets de notre propre misère

Poetics of Islands

I could have written poetically of the islands since they draw our destiny with their constellations on the ocean; I could have spoken from the heart of this resonance, the sound of water on the senses, forgetting that their volcanic earth and basalt roots are all that anchor them and keep them from drifting out to sea, that they hold in them the stamp of time, of the ages, of people sanded down, the people we have become.

And then again no.

I have no business writing the poetics of the islands. Of the tea trees, their sublime homeopathy, of the deceptive blue of our skies, the lean and slender music of the bird-flutes of our sinister shepherds, our bait that waits like little girls, open-mouthed to infinity

I'm sick of biting off and chewing this dust, of scratching with my thin claws, searching for some chunk of literary gold

to hell with all the disarrayed images of our homelands

reflections of our particular misery

images gravitationnelles qui nous lestent de trop de nous-mêmes et nous condamnent à rôder le nez au sol, au ras des terres tondues au vitriol

images de nous-mêmes qui nous font pleurer de l'infinie petitesse de nos songes

Et de ne pouvoir : en faire plus, en dire plus, que les mots n'aient un autre chapeau, quelque chose comme une incandescence, une sorte de brûlure, qu'ils n'aient plus aucun pouvoir que celui de se taire, sauf, évidemment, si l'on parle du haut d'une chaire au nom d'un dieu quelconque ou à l'abri d'une plate-forme—que de suffrages brigués parmi les décombres, que d'espérances semées à coups de matraque

Non—les autres—les mots décortiqués comme un ver nu, qui enlacent comme les bras multipliés d'un banian, mots chargés d'usure métallique et angélique de vie de mort de rictus de rêves de désabus, l'écriture comme on ne s'en souvenait plus, mais ces mots-là ne vont pas plus loin que le bout de mes doigts, s'enlisent d'ombre et d'amnésie, se dispersent aussitôt dits, vont au cimetière marin des naufragés ou parmi les cadavres d'éléphants morts en perdant leurs défenses

gravitational images that weigh us down with too much self and condemn us to keep our noses to the ground, to the acid-razed earth

images of us made to weep by the infinite smallness of our dreams

And being unable: to say more, to do more, that the words can't wear another hat, something incandescent, a sort of burning, that they have no other power except to remain silent unless one speaks from the pulpit in the name of some god or from the podium, so many votes lobbied among the ruins like hopes scattered by the lash of billy clubs

No—the others—words dissected like worms which slither and twist like branches of a banyan tree, words charged with angelic and metallic use, by life by death by the lurid leers of dreams by disillusionment, writing like one can't remember any more, but the words don't travel any farther than the tips of my fingers, stuck in darkness and amnesia, dispersing as soon as they are spoken, gone to the shipwrecked sailors' cemetery, or amid the graveyard of the elephants who died losing their tusks

Qu'y pouvons-nous, nous qui n'avons rien d'autre que cela, que les mots pour penser pour traduire pour assurer pour trahir que des mots qui ne déboucheront jamais que sur l'indifférence et ce n'est pas peu dire sauf s'ils s'accompagnent de menaces, là on écoute, terrorisme du verbe, pourquoi pas, mais l'écriture n'a jamais convaincu au moyen de menaces ni de réponses, seulement des questions, des interrogations, des pourquoi, des comment, on ne sait pas dire parce que parce que l'on sait qu'on ne sait rien tout ce que l'on peut faire c'est vous dire demandez-vous s'il y a d'autres réponses que celles du prédicateur, du prédicteur, de l'imprécateur, dites-vous que seuls comptent votre jugement et votre vérité, pourquoi toujours écouter et croire ce qu'on vous dit, surtout ces images téléguidées pardon télévisées sans lesquelles vous êtes perdus comme des enfants et ne comprenez plus grand-chose, vous ne connaissez plus le nom des choses, ni arbre, ni chaise, ni visage, vous avez besoin qu'on vous le dise noir sur blanc, ceci est un arbre ceci est une chaise ceci n'est pas un homme ceci est une femme qui a fauté lancez-lui la pierre des mots et délivrez-vous du mal

Comment dans ces circonstances dites-le moi

Comment voulez-vous

Comment ne pas entrer en état de rage comme on entre en état de grâce

What can we do, we don't have anything other than words to think to translate to certify to betray words that lead nowhere but indifference and have never been spoken except when accompanied by a threat, and when we listen, terrorisms of words, why not, but writing never convinced with threats nor answers, only with questions, interrogations, the whys and hows you cannot tell because because you know you know nothing at all, all that one can do is to say ask yourself if there are other responses than those of a preacher, a fortune teller, a doomsayer, you should realize only your own judgement and truthfulness matter, why do you always believe everything you hear, all the images remote-controlled into you, oh excuse me, televized into you without which you would be lost like children and never understand anything important, you don't even know the names of things any more, not a tree, not a chair, a face, you need someone to tell you what is white and what is black, this is a tree, this is a chair, this isn't a man this is a woman who has gone bad throw a stone of words and deliver yourself from evil

Tell me how in these circumstances

How can you possibly

How can you not enter a state of rage like entering a state of grace

Puis on voit l'aile l'ombre d'un feu follet des quartiers pauvres, un trait de lumière, une gifle de pluie, un rayon brun-noir, puis on le suit pour savoir où il va pour ne pas le perdre de vue comprendre sa lumière et son rire, s'y accrocher, tant qu'il y a cela il y aura ceci, l'espoir, puis on voit où il va où il s'enfonce et là on sait que lui non plus n'aura pas

Comment parler à cet enfant, oui, lui, là, qui fait le fanfaron devant les caméras, ce gamin des rues au corps frêle et nerveux aux mollets durs et footeux à tant courir sur les pavés, au rire grand clair blanc qui s'estompe lorsque soudain descend sur ses épaules sur sa nuque délicate et pensive sur son dos lisse le pouvoir

Pouvoir de vie et de mort lorsqu'il se réveille un jour, l'insouciance éclatée par une Kalachnikov descendue entre ses mains

Et la vie prend une autre couleur, un autre metal

Comment lui dire, à lui, ce gamin-là, qui aurait pu être le mien, que ce n'est pas la seule voie qu'il y en a d'autres que tu peux, si tu veux, passer outre ces élans explosifs, le pouvoir mensonger d'une balle désinvolte parce qu'au moment où tu te crois prêt à le recevoir, à l'assumer, à prendre ton destin en main, il t'échappe, volte-face avec dédain et te touche en pleine figure, le coup tu ne le vois pas venir mais de ta lèvre éclatée pend la boue de tes rêves et puis avec ça aux mains tu ne connaîtras des autres que leur peur tu les plieras à ta rage mais aucun corps ne te sera offert dans l'amour

Then you see a wing, a flickering shadow of a will-o'-wisp in the poor neighbourhoods, a stroke of light, a slap of rain, a brown-black ray, then you follow it to find out where it goes to not lose sight of it to understand what you've seen, his light and his laugh, to hang on to him, as long as he will be there you'll have hope, then you see where he goes, where he buries himself and where you know he will no longer be

How to speak to this child, yes, him, 'there' the one who brags before the cameras, this young street kid with the slender body and strong sinewy calves from so much running on the pavement, with a loud clear laugh fading suddenly away down through his shoulders, his delicate neck, his smooth back, the power

Power of life and death until he wakes up one day, his carefree careless ways shot down by a Kalashnikov dropped into his hands

And life takes on a different shade, a different metal

How to tell him, this kid who could have been mine, that this isn't the only way that there are others you can choose if you want, pass past these explosive impulses, the deceptive casual power of a bullet, because at the moment you think yourself ready to receive it, to take on your destiny by the hand, it will escape you, contemptuous reversal and strike you right in the face, the killing blow you do not see coming but from your exploded mouth hangs the mud of your dreams and with this in your hands you will know nothing of the others but their fear you will bend by your rage but no other body will have ever offered you love

73

Que gagneras-tu? Rien qu'une mort désolée et ignominieuse avant même que d'avoir vécu avant même que d'avoir su les vastes possibles les alléchants probables tu es un petit tas moribond et l'air craché de ta bouche est le dernier

Crois-tu que ceux qui parviennent au pouvoir en grimpant sur ton dos se souviendront de ton petit visage de lune et de soleil

de ton rire étoilé

de ton nez plissé de colère

de tes mains souples comme des anguilles?

Rien du tout, même pas du bruit de leurs semelles dans ton dos. Petit couteau prompt à te glisser dans un ventre, tu te retourneras bientôt contre toi-même. Tu ne comptes pas plus que ça.

Je voudrais te tenir dans mes bras. Te bercer et te rendre à l'enfant que tu es, caresser tes dorures
lorsqu'elles brûlent, souffler un chant de sommeil dans ta bouche lorsque l'ennui te ronge. Je voudrais être celle qui te miracle. Te sortir de l'urgence pour te rendre à l'innocence et à l'insolence, contempler l'endormissement de tes jambes écartées, de tes bras jetés, de ta tête renversée, cela ressemble à une mort mais ça ne l'est pas, c'est autre chose, c'est la tempête d'un rêve passé en trombe sur tes voiles, c'est une trêve feuillue mâchée entre tes dents et qui a un goût de liberté.

What will you gain? Nothing but a lonely death and an ignominious one even before having lived even before having known the vast possibilities the many temptations you are a little dead heap and the air spitting out of your mouth is your last

Do you think those who gain power climbing on your back will remember the little sun and moon of your face

your starry laughter

your nose wrinkling in anger

your hands flexible as eels?

None of it, not even the sound of their boots treading on your back

A little knife, ready to slide into a belly, you will turn soon enough against yourself. You don't matter to them any more than that.

I want to take you in my arms. Rock you like the child you are, caress your gilt edges when they burn, whisper a lullaby in your mouth until ordinariness settles in you. I want to be the one who saves you. Draws you from the urgent need to give you back innocence and insolence, contemplates your sleeping limbs, legs splayed out, your arms thrown wide, your head slumped to one side, all this looks like death, but it's not death, it's another thing, the storm of a dream passing in a downpour against your sails, a leafy respite in your mouth, tasting of freedom.

Le gamin s'est enfui. Il n'a que faire de moi. Je dois le laisser partir. Il va rejoindre les milices, la seduction d'une bannière. Dans son pays, on récupère des mots de poésie et on en fait une boucherie. Il en est ainsi des chimères. Chacun de nos dieux nous murmure à l'oreille ses paroles incantatoires. S'il nous dit de tuer, faut-il l'écouter? Jusqu'où ira cette obédience?

The kid fled. He didn't want anything to do with me. I had to let him leave. He will rejoin his militia, the seduction of a flag. In his country, they take the words of poetry and turn them into butchery. Such is the fate of chimeras. Each one of our gods whispers into our ears its own incantatory lines. If we are told to kill, should we listen? Until when do we continue this obedience?

Peaux

Premiers pas, porte entrouverte, corps lourds de leur encombrement. Rires bêtes. Après vous, non, vous avant. Rires bêtes. Regards appuyés. Fesses? Seins? Sexe? Yeux jauges plus rapides que les balances électroniques. Oui, après tout, il ne s'agit que de ça.

La chambre est louée pour une heure. Pas beaucoup de temps pour les préliminaires. Il faut du temps pour les faux-semblants. Ici, on ne paie pas en espèces. On paie en promesses. D'un avenir radieux mort avant d'exister.

Draps tirés mais incertitude de propreté.

Peaux d'un soir vierges de cendre noire surplombant sans les voir les cierges du mouroir

Peaux du sort dés jetés au plat des corps carénés à l'équerre de passions minutées noeud coulant des
obédiences longitude brisée et pudeur animale

Peaux de vie eau de coeur extraite de sarments juteux et de serments douteux d'évidences dénouées comme une lente tresse qui ne saurait masquer la détresse d'un corps flasque et lanciné

Skin

First steps, partly open door, bodies burdened. Dumb laughter. After you, no you first. A glance. Dumb laughter. Buttocks? Breasts? Crotch? Eyes quickly balance the accounts. Yes, after all, it doesn't get better than this.

The room is free for an hour. Not much time for preliminaries. You need time for false pretence. Here, you don't pay in kind. It's all drawn on promises. To a radiant future over even before you've begun.

Sheets of uncertain cleanliness pulled back.

Evening skin, virgin black ash hanging in the air over unseen candles of the dying

Skin of fate dice thrown flat on a body careening squared by timed passions and strung by obedience broken longitude and animal modesty

Skin of life water from the heart drawn from succulent vines and dubious vows evidence unfolding like untwisting plait of hair that cannot hide the despair of the body throbbing and limp

Ils passent, ils passent, ne cessent de passer, jamais ne s'attardent, le vent le veut ainsi, qui disperse si vite les poussières de peau et la cire des surfaces, ils vont d'un seul rythme mais ont deux voix, l'obscurité leur masque le vide du second pas, ils sombrent, ils tombent, vite réduits à eux-mêmes et ce n'est pas assez, le bruit que vous faites en dormant est celui du temps et vos interstices abritent leur défaite qui attend pour sortir la commissure de dégoût et le jaune d'après-amour, et que vienne la crainte du moment suivant dans leur regard fuyant où soudain les ombres ricanent

Peaux illusoires à quoi sert-il de tant déguiser la duplicité et de leur faire croire à vos aires accueillantes?

Les peaux plus que tout autre se nourrissent de l'odeur de pourriture qui affleure des passions aussitôt consommées.

Peaux ventrales mais non maternelles, aux aveux impitoyables— faims de rites et de siècles et d'obscurité exaspérée, aube tombale.

Peaux que l'on arrache pour mieux siroter la concupiscence et braver l'impuissance des fins annoncées sitôt les passions nées, rien ne montre mieux le chemin que l'amour.

Rien, autant que le crissement d'une peau contre l'autre, ne permet mieux d'entendre le sourire de la mort.

They pass and pass, never cease passing, that's what the wind wants, that so quickly disperses dust of skins and wax of surfaces, they move to a single rhythm but have two voices, the darkness hides the emptiness of the second step, they sink, they fall, dissipating swiftly, and it's not enough, the sound you make sleeping is the sound of time itself and your chinks hide the defeat that waits to leave the corner of your mouth in disgust and the jaundiced aftermath and the dread that follows in the fleeting and sudden glances where shadows jeer

Illusory skin why disguise your duplicity and pretend welcome spaces await?

Skin, more than anything, feeds off the smell of decay that rises from swiftly spent passions.

Skin sagging and unmaternal, of merciless confessions, ritual hungers, and eras of anger and dark, funereal dawn.

Skin that one peels back the better to suck the craving and brave the powerlessness of endings foretold as soon as passion is born, nothing carves the path better than love.

Nothing, so much as the grinding of skin against skin, allows one to hear better the laughter of death.

Translator's Note

An Interview with Ananda Devi

Reading Devi's Poetry

Insights
Interviews &
More...

Translator's Note

Kazim Ali

I picked up the small book *Quand la nuit consent à me parler* in a
Paris bookstore en route to India. While in the French district of
Puducherry I began reading the poems and almost immediately I
found myself translating the book in my head. Their language is
clear and direct, but it is a clarity of surface that belies the depth of
darkness and feeling within them. At some point, I began writing
the translations down in my book. Devi has the habit, which I do
not have, of speaking hard truths plainly. Putting her words into
(through?) my mouth changed the contours of my own expression
and I am not sure that I am yet grateful for the gift of being able to
transmit emotions one might term 'negative'—anger, frustration,
despair—into poetry. Certainly, the poems of my own that I was
writing alongside this task of translation assumed a different
dimension than I had previously been capable of.

It was less karaoke and more full-blown drag.

From Puducherry, I travelled to Kerala, and there, sitting on
the cliffs of Varkala overlooking the sun-stunned width of the
Arabian Sea, I found myself finishing the translations which had
begun as a poet's way of understanding the text better. It's true that
I struggled mightily to carry over the subtlest turns of phrase and
the most seemingly delicate of images. Devi's poetry only *appears*
on the page to be plain-spoken and direct. Within that apparent

simplicity lie fathoms upon fathoms of meaning. I found in that town overlooking the Indian Ocean the truth of Devi's ferocity—that it progresses from deep tenderness and vulnerability.

Indeed the translation of this book was a bridge from one kind of poetry to another for me as well. I thank Ananda Devi, who has been very supportive and read the translations and offered many comments, large and small. Alexis Bernaut also read original drafts and gave critical feedback, particularly on the three short prose pieces that close the collection.

In poetry and translation both, the borders between writer, translator and reader are porous and multidirectional. So I must acknowledge a sideways debt to Cristina Peri Rossi, whose book *Evohe* I was translating concurrently with this one—they are both books about the body, about women's bodies, though very different from one another—books of desire both terrifying and dizzying, one by a woman in the first moments of her sexual liberation and the other by a woman with a lifetime of painful experiences. In passing them through *my* body I find myself both charged and changed.

An Interview with Ananda Devi

Kazim Ali: What is your relationship to language? As someone who speaks several—that I know of, English, French, and Mauritian Creole—do you have a relationship to a 'mother tongue'? What are the possibilities that French offers to your writing? Have you ever written in another language and how did that impact the writing itself?

Ananda Devi: You have started out with the most difficult question because it is so close to my heart, and painful in a visceral way. I am indeed trilingual: I am equally fluent in French, Mauritian Creole and English, and I can understand Hindi and German. But I should have been fluent in *four* languages: the very first language my mother spoke to me was Telugu. I heard it and spoke it for maybe the first three years of my life, along with Creole. In the village where I lived, people also spoke Bhojpuri. As soon as I went to preschool, I started learning French and English. These were the two languages I began to read and write in. Gradually, all these languages took over from Telugu, because my mother was the only one who spoke this language to me. As children tend to do, I adopted the languages of my peers and that would make me feel I belonged. I very soon stopped responding to my mother and gradually lost Telugu completely.

Since I started to write at a very young age, around seven/eight years old, first in English and French and then almost exclusively in French, the loss of Telugu did not seem so important to me until one day, as an adult, I was forced to face this void. For it is indeed a void. The loss of the mother tongue is the exact opposite of the presence of a baby in a mother's womb: it is a hollowing out, a tearing apart, an uprooting of something that had so strongly, so powerfully connected these two bodies, these two people, these two lives. Perhaps I avoided thinking about it in order not to understand that it might have been a rejection not only of the language, but also of my mother? I only came to understand much later that this had been a source of pain for her... After her death, this led to an inner conviction that I had betrayed her. And there would be no way of making it up to her. I have to go on living with it. Luckily for me, writing has always been this place where I could find myself, however lost I was. And French is so close to my heart, to my mind, to my emotions and senses and even to my subconscious that it offered me a deep and intimate consolation. I do not really miss Telugu as a language: I miss my mother's voice in this language.

KA: You translated one of your books but haven't done that since. Can you explain what that process was like and whether you would try to do this again? Considering the multiple languages that exist in places like Mauritius and India, including the presences of local languages and colonial languages alongside one another, how do the politics of translation function in such multilingual societies?

AD: Apart from being a writer I am also a translator. So, it would have been natural for me to translate my books into English and/

or Creole myself. Incidentally, I could have become an English-language writer just as easily as I became a French-language writer, since it wasn't a matter of choice but of inclination in my early teenage years. Somehow, French became predominant, perhaps because of a deep resonance it had with the poetry I wanted to write, and its musicality and lyricism corresponded to my way of writing and were closer to the Urdu ghazals I listened to and whose rhythms found their way into my cadences. So, to come back to translation, I really felt the need to do it after writing *Pagli*, in 2000, when I became so attached to the characters that I didn't want to leave them. So, I started immediately rewriting it in English. Then, the French Institute of Delhi organized a book tour for me in India, including the Jaipur Literature Festival, and they wanted to have one of my books published in English in India. I proposed my own translation of *Pagli*, which was published by Rupa Publishers in 2007. I loved the entire process, and how the musicality of the language influenced the way I was translating myself and taking liberties with my own text. But afterwards, I thought that having another translator's eye on the original was more important, because the adaptation process is essential, with all the cultural subtext that is involved in making a text readable in the receiving culture. I wasn't wrong in this: all the books that were translated by other translators have given me something back, a kind of insight into my own work, a mirror, in fact, which reflected what I had written, but with something more: the palimpsest of another language, another culture, but also of another writer.

Another exercise in self-translation was for the poems entitled *Ceux du large*, about the migrant experience. In this case, I wrote the poems in French and rewrote them in Creole and English, and all three versions were published in the same book by my publisher. This was deliberate, as I wanted these texts to reach out to all my possible readers because of the urgency of this subject (I wrote them in 2016, and translated the poems into English while in the US during Trump's electoral campaign), and it has become even more urgent since. It is with a deep despair that I say this.

Concerning the politics of translation, strangely enough, Mauritius, with its myriad languages, has never been a place where writers were widely or even commonly translated. It was as if each language had its readership and that it sufficed. I wrote in French, and so my Mauritian readership was wider than for writers in other languages, including English, because even those who commonly speak Creole or English or Hindi do read French. If I had written in Creole, paradoxically, my readership would have been almost nonexistent even though it is the spoken language of ninety-nine per cent of Mauritians! This is because Creole is considered, even today, a 'subaltern' language, a sub-language derived from French under French colonization and in the context of slavery. Yet, because of this fact, it is a language that should be upheld by all Mauritians as the language of their freedom and rebellion from colonization! There are writers who write in Creole, and I do too, but unfortunately, even those who should be able to read these texts do not do so because they find the phonetic spelling difficult to read.

Does this mean that Mauritian writers should not write in English and French (the languages of the colonizers) or even Hindi (India is after all a major power that has exercised its politics in Mauritius for many decades)? I don't think so because when I write in French, it is my language, I have appropriated it, I have transformed it into something different, I have infused it with Creole and Urdu and English. A writer's language is not about politics: it's her lifeblood.

KA: You write in various genres—fiction, poetry, autobiographical prose—and this book, *When the Night Agrees to Speak to Me*, combines poetry and prose. What is your relationship to the genre? How would you characterize the prose pieces in this book?

AD: I have always written a *prose poétique*, i.e., poetic prose, and sometimes prose poems. In fact, the demarcation between the two is a very loose one for me, since my early writing years. As a teenager, I used to switch from short stories to novels to poetry to plays without feeling I had to stick to one genre. But gradually, I began to concentrate on prose, first short stories, then novels. I did not publish any poetry for a long time, mainly because I think it is the most difficult genre, but also because for me poetry arises from a kind of burst, a fulgurance of emotions, which means that I can write an entire series in a few days, and when the burst dies down, a few years will elapse before the next. But all my writing is linked by a poetic flow that I need to find even in my novels. In this book, *When the Night Agrees to Speak to Me,* the first part consists of poems I wrote in the kind of burst I was talking about, and it is autobiographical in that I was going through a difficult period of my life, with questions as to who I was as a woman, a mother, a wife, and the only thing keeping me sane was immersing myself in the act of writing. The voices of the absent resonate deeply in these poems, because as you grow older, you feel these absences more strongly, and it also feels like you are placing your own feet in their departing, dwindling footsteps. There is a need to think back on your own life, the good memories as well as the sorrows and regrets. There is a terrible pain in these lines:

> *That my tomorrow be a yesterday*
> *Since nothing is left to accomplish*
> *Nothing to build or to destroy*
> *Nothing has already become: Never*

I am in a better place now, but these lines still echo in my mind and body, an unceasing knell.

At the same time, there was also the wider arena of political turmoil around me, and in 'Words Die a Slow Death' I wanted to address what was happening outside the sphere of intimacy: Nicolas Sarkozy was the French President at that time, and the way he sometimes used vulgar words in public (he told a member of the public who refused to shake his hand 'Casse-toi, pauvre con!'—'Get lost, asshole!') made me want to write about the importance of words, and how writers have to think about each word they write, weigh their meaning and their importance, whereas public figures could bandy the most banal or vulgar words without compunction, with a feeling of immunity and power. So in the French version of this piece, I used *pauvres complices, pauvres conjurés, pauvres convaincus* as a way to reproduce the *pauvre con* used by Sarkozy, but obviously in a subverting way.

The second prose piece is about the way young boys in islands such as Haiti are transformed into little warriors because of poverty and politics, and the modern slavery that poor countries are subjected to, and again, it is a way of expressing a kind of rage about the human condition, rage against the times, rage against the selling-out of those who could help, and how it is only the weak who suffer, who have to pay the price. Nothing has changed since I wrote this book. It is even worse now.

The third piece is less political, but perhaps not so much. It's about male–female politics, if you wish, about sensuality and sexuality and the beauty of a caress and the disguise of our skin and what is revealed beneath. In the end, the skin hides the rotting that goes on beneath, and is the only armour against death.

KA: The long title poem of this book is in thirty pieces, which begs a comparison to the lunar month or to the menstrual cycle (or both!). Would you situate this as specifically woman-centred or gendered writing? How might you situate your writing in the contexts of the French literary movements of *l'écriture féminine* or *le nouveau roman* or other global literary movements or feminisms?

AD: In my novels, I try to divest myself of all identity, becoming whoever my narrator is, including the eighty-year-old violent misogynist of *Le sari vert*. However, poetry for me is different because it is more personal and intimate, and far more autobiographical. And so, yes, you could say that the first thirty poems are woman-centred, and even if not deliberately reflecting the menstrual cycle, this number probably does so, subconsciously, because menstrual blood is so present in most of my writings both symbolically, as in *Pagli*, and graphically, as in *Eve Out of Her Ruins*. However, I would not consider myself to be part of any movement, and specifically not of any French literary movement. *Le nouveau roman* has had its day, although I tremendously admire Marguerite Duras. Auto-fiction, which is another French trend that has held sway in recent years is not a trend I would necessarily follow—when I wrote about myself in *Les hommes qui me parlent*, I did so without disguising the text as fiction. I don't think there is any movement at all in writing today. Every writer follows their own inclination, and I think this is a good thing. Movements are there to be followed. Writing is an individualistic act in which one questions everything.

I do, however, consider myself a feminist. When I was young I tended to reject all types of labels. But I have come to reconsider this because feminism is necessary, still, in our times. And not only feminism; we need to speak out against racism, against the rejection of homosexuality and different sexuality, against casteism, against all kinds of discrimination. It is after all what I have been writing about all this time. The rejection of difference is what turns people into monsters. So, in my books there is no Manichaeism, no black-and-white or good-and-evil tropes, there is only the ambiguity of people, and it is up to the readers to come to their own conclusions and answers; but in my life, I will always speak out and stand for those whom their difference has turned into outcasts. The novel I am working on right now is set in India and narrated by a Hijra. It was totally unexpected. But somehow natural.

KA: Your work has sometimes been placed in conversation with that of other francophone postcolonial writers, such as Kim Thúy, Mariama Bâ, Maryse Condé, or Vénus Khoury-Ghata, to name a few. Do you feel a particular affinity to this global tradition? What does it mean to you now to publish in India? If there is a relationship to French or Mauritian writing and forms in your work, are there ways in which you also feel connections to the history, literature, or languages of India? Are there Indian or Indian-Diaspora Anglophone poets to whom you feel resonance?

AD: I was immensely privileged to be born in Mauritius: I grew up literally at the confluence of cultures (this might sound as a cliché, but it isn't). Even before I could read, my mother would relate the tales of the Ramayana and the Mahabharata to me (with a feminist bent that I only came to understand much later). My father read the tales of Grimm and Perrault, and taught me the alphabet when I was three years old. We heard the music of different continents on the radio and, later on, on television. I studied the piano for a few years and came to love Western classical music passionately. I also studied kathak for a few years and grew to love Indian classical music and dance. I watched Bollywood movies and French avant-garde. I discovered African writers from the age of fifteen and my feeling of proximity with them in every way has never waned. So, I feel as if I belong to all traditions (I have lived in Congo-Brazzaville and am now living in France; when I am in India I am taken for an Indian, whether in the north or the south, until I say I can't speak the language), and sometimes, as if I belong to none. If I had to choose, I would say my proximity with African writing is the closest of all. We've gone through the same colonial rules, slavery is part of our history, and the independence of our countries came at around the same time. We expressed this in our writing, and for many of us through the French language. And so, yes, today I have many close friends from the African continent, including a kind of male muse with whom I have engaged in a literary dialogue for the past twenty years. But at the same time, I feel the resonance with many other writers, irrespective of history or geography. Each writer's literary family transcends place and time.

KA: Your poems engage with alienation, loneliness, desire, violence, aging, and contending with family hierarchies. How does one contend with such challenging and raw subject matter?

AD: Only when one gets older! I am only partly facetious. What I mean to say is that you need to have the experience of half a lifetime behind you to even begin to address some of these issues. When you are young, you think that everything can change. When you grow older, you realize that you yourself have to change, to understand that all of it is part of life's experience, that life is not about pursuing happiness but about coming to terms: with who you are, with what you've done, with what was not possible, with what is still possible. I couldn't have written about all this at twenty or thirty. Even at forty, I was still struggling to become the writer I wanted to be. But at fifty, you start looking back and understanding. And accepting. Regrets will always be there, but you learn to live with them. Earlier this year, my latest book of poetry came out. It's entitled *Danser sur tes braises* (*Dancing on Your Embers*). The first part is about my mother. She died in 1993. It's only now that I have been able to put into words everything I felt about her. The second part is entitled *Six décennies* (*Six Decades*). It is, obviously, about aging, about my having reached this point, and what it does to the female body, and what desires still burn in it. And so, yes, this subject matter is challenging, but writing is challenging. You challenge yourself all the time when you write. And this is what makes it interesting for me: how far can I push myself?

KA: *When the Night Agrees to Speak to Me* draws equally from an extremely physical sense of carnality/incarnation in its focus on the body, yet—as its title indicates—it depends very much on a spiritual engagement with what is beyond the human, what could, in a sense, be thought of as divine. How does this dual lineage of spirit and body develop throughout this book and your work in general?

AD: I have never believed in the separation of body and spirit. So, absolutely, carnality/incarnation are an indication that we are both physical, and at the same time an incarnation of everything else because when we die we become part of a whole. No atom is wasted. Whether we burn or rot or are devoured by vultures, we very literarily return to nature. This is why I both believe in our spiritual being, in our continuity beyond our temporal life, and disbelieve religions, which harness our reason to unquestioning faith. The idea that a superior being that created us (possible) would discriminate between us (questionable) is ludicrous. Religion has simply become another power play, another means of discrimination. I do not subscribe with the books written by men (and I mean men in the gendered sense) with their decrees as coming from God. I believe in an inherent morality that makes us respect others, including other species, and that does not rely on blind faith. If human beings have acquired the capacity of reasoning, it is not to abandon this capacity on the say-so of century-old beliefs. It is to question everything and to derive our own principles and morality. Is this what we are seeing today? Emphatically no! We have enslaved ourselves to the gods of money, of power, of class, of caste, of looks, etc.

All the major religions see the female body as the source of temptation and sin. If I am menstruating or pregnant, I cannot walk into a temple. I need to be hidden, kept away, bedridden or whatever. What does this say to me? That men wrote these rules and were afraid of the female body, in particular procreation, which was denied to them. Male domination harks back to our biological origins. But women need to be in control of their body. Sexuality isn't a sin, and abstinence or monogamy are not linked to some kind of purity. These are matters of individual choice. It is the exercise of power and dominance, the twin sins of all human civilization, that have led to where we are today: women can't walk alone in India and in many other places without the fear of being raped. Teaching women to defend themselves is a possibility. Teaching men not to rape is a necessity. And by this, I don't mean that all men will end up raping women. I mean that teaching respect of women and of every other human being as well as all living things, including our planet, from infanthood onward is essential. But perhaps we have learned this lesson too late for any possibility of redemption.

Conducted over email. August 2020

Reading Devi's Poetry

Mohit Chandna

Her prolific writing across genres might have won her many awards and attracted much critical acclaim, but the reason why Ananda Devi stands today at the forefront of postcolonial literature is the viable alternative identity paradigm that she proposes in the male-dominated francophone literary canon. How to articulate the history of Mauritius, an island that saw the arrival of the colonizers—the Dutch, the French and the English—the accompanying slaves from Africa, and thereafter the indentured labourers from India and China, is already a complex enough question. As she weighs various identity paradigms to find an answer to it, it is the firm voice with which she asserts her own identity of a woman of Indian origins, and counters the patriarchal and casteist hierarchies of the Hindu religion, that gives Devi's oeuvre its unique quality. Death, rebirth, reincarnation, shared histories and a sense of inhabiting a community of women are among the motifs that one discovers in her writing, be it short stories, novels or her poetry.

Devi's book of poems, *When the Night Agrees to Speak to Me,* takes on a woman's voice to address the reader. In relating the moment ('when') of consent to 'speak', the title of this collection presents speech and carries within it the absence of speech that preceded it. Devi, after all, is faced with writing about the impossibility of communicating the abject human exploitation, that too in the very French language that served to subjugate the colonized populations of Mauritius.

Appearing towards the end of the collection, the poem 'Words Die a Slow Death', in displaying how 'words erect walls of lies', might seem to be about such an impossibility of language. However, when this poem deploys language to underline its own limitations, it is putting into action a process of harnessing poetry-writing to bypass the inabilities of human language. Since it provides us a way out of a linguistic cul-de-sac by speaking of the simultaneity of speech and non-speech present in the title 'When the Night Agrees to Speak to Me', one understands why poetry figures in this poem, and indeed throughout this collection, as 'our vein'.

In her insistence on 'poetics', Devi shares much with other well-known concepts in the francophone literary tradition. Through allusions to similar articulations, such as *Poétique de la Relation* (*Poetics of Relation*) by Édouard Glissant, Devi enters into a dialogue to set up her own voice. Just as some renditions of Négritude unambiguously situate their origins in Africa, many writers belonging to the diaspora of slavery and indentured labour display similar yearnings to locate geographical origins in their quest for an identity. In her poem 'The Poetics of Islands', Devi is, no doubt, retorting against such a geographically tied understanding of identity when she emphatically states: 'to hell with all the disarrayed images of our homelands'. This indictment of homeland and similar '[g]ravitational images', are an acknowledgement of the reductive nature of such identity paradigms that 'weigh us down with too much selves'. In other words, these paradigms do not recognize the complex, multifaceted nature of identity construction that makes any anchoring unachievable.

This would explain why Devi constantly beckons the reader, as she does in the ninth poem, to 'Peel back my skin. Unclothe me of myself. / Look closer', and then confronts the reader with instances that show the lack of identity, or rather an inarticulable identity. A 'green sari' (evocative no doubt of Devi's prize-winning novel, *Le sari vert*), the very garment that a woman covers herself with, exercises indifference towards her and indicates instead her erasure. Confronted with this erasure, the reader understands how any attempts at locating identity, in particular a woman's identity, can only mark a site of absence, as do the following lines: 'An unrolled swathe of green sari / Indifferent to the lot / Of a woman erased / By her bruises'.

Even as stabilizing the complexities of identity remains an impossible task, this insistent invitation to attempt definitions of this opaque presence is what sets apart Devi's poetry and identity politics in the mostly male-centric, origin-fixated postcolonial francophone canon, dominated until recently by those like Léopold Sédar Senghor (Senegal), and Léon-Gontran Damas (French Guiana).[1] For only in such an enunciation can we understand how poetry, identity and language cannot exist

---

1   For more, read Anne M. François, *Rewriting the Return to Africa: Voices of Francophone Caribbean Women Writers*, Lexington Books, 2011.

as separate entities but as entwined in a mutually influencing relationship. They must forever be perceived as part of a multilayered process that is constantly evolving. Once we realize that we write in the awareness of violence and in the presence of its colonial fallout; that we can never have access to the lost voices of those subjugated, nor ever have words to describe the accompanying exploitation; that any attempts at trying to authorize a definitive voice is impossible; only then can we appreciate why having a conversation with 'voices of those absent' is only possible in the dark of the night, where both the speaker and the interlocutor not only remain forever aware of a presence, but also forever unable to recognize each other.

* * *

'It was less karaoke and more like full-blown drag.'—Kazim Ali, writes in his Note on translating Ananda Devi's poetry.

It took me some time to understand why Kazim Ali, while recalling his experience of translating Devi's poetry, called it 'full-blown drag'. I was convinced that it had to be more than the facile explanation of seeing the act of translation as an attempt at singing along and thus assuming subservience to the original text.

The idea of 'drag' also explains the workings of gender in human society. Gender, much like drag, is nothing but a constant imitation of the dominant norm. While 'drag' is definitely in conversation with questions of gender identity as they appear in Devi's poetry, I remained convinced that 'drag' was also about something else. I soon discovered that what Ali said was central to capturing Devi's multilayered complexity; it displayed his deep understanding of the importance of language in her poetry. Ali so ably renders these poems into English that I couldn't help but wonder if it was because he is himself an award-winning novelist and poet, or, like Devi, he too is of Indian origins, or, perhaps because having spent his life in different parts of the world, he understands better the concepts of rootedness and migration in a writer's life. The answer to that question might not be as relevant as acknowledging the sheer pleasure that one derives in reading the poetry in this collection. It could not have found a better translator.

The already difficult task of rendering into English Devi's lyrical and rhythmic French is made even more so for this collection whose title demands attention to the materiality of speech ('speak'). The opening poem presents 'Your ears [that] strain to hear' and prepares the reader for a poetry that needs to be read, and read out aloud of course, but even more importantly, also heard very carefully. After such a diktat, one only imagines the translator's dilemma with a poem such as 'Words Die a Slow Death'. This poem lauds poetry's function of empowering language by reimagining and reinventing its boundaries. Without poetry, human language would be no more than a 'skeleton of silence'. This poem not only states that poetry enriches language but through its own structures it renders this into reality.

The French title of the poem in original, 'Les mots meurent de mort lente', as well as phrases such as 'sens ensevelis' and 'tournures troubles' are just a few of the numerous examples of the assonance and the alliteration available in this poem. A cursory first reading also reveals that the absence of punctuation is adding to the semantic ambiguity forcing the reader to perpetually reconstitute meaning. The reason Ali's translation works isn't just because he successfully 'karaokes' Devi at moments like 'sense unsensed' and 'troubled turns'. It is also because, in a collection where questions of language and nation-based identities are intertwined, when confronted with choosing between the two meanings of 'notre voix', he unhesitatingly retains both by translating 'notre voix' as 'our voices our votes'.

That Ali rehearses Judith Butler, who too uses drag to exemplify the normative formation of gendered identities, becomes even clearer in seeing his response as a translator to the word 'langue', which in French means both language and tongue. The word appears twice: 'tournures troubles d'une langue explorant des pays carmin sans elle la langue ne reçoit'. And, predictably, 'langue' opens up the possibility of a multitude of semantic permutations and combinations. However, unlike with 'voix', where Ali retains both voices and votes, for 'langue' Ali alternates between the two meanings. He chooses 'tongue' first and then 'language' for the second usage of langue: 'troubled turns of tongue exploring carmine countries without it language receives'. It is precisely because he alternates between these two meanings that Ali can stay alongside Devi's musicality, and also successfully read Devi via Butler.

In speaking of how normative gender is formed, Butler elaborates on a 'hegemonic heterosexuality'[2] that remains in

---

2   Judith Butler, 'Gender is Burning: Questions of Appropriation and Subversion', in *Dangerous Liaisons: Gender, Nation and*

'constant and repeated effort to imitate its own idealizations'. In her much-anthologized essay, 'Gender is Burning', Butler states: to 'claim that all gender is like drag, or is drag, is to suggest that "imitation" is at the heart of the *heterosexual* project and its gender binarism'. In other words, gender does not exist 'prior to its constructions' and its meaning is stabilized by constant reiterations. Drag, with its insistence on imitation, is meant to situate this 'hegemonic heterosexuality' as a function of what it establishes as ideal gendered behaviour.

As much as drag testifies to the heteronormative rules it imitates, it is also the very site that provides for the means of rewriting the text of gender. For us, while discussing Devi's work and Ali's translation, it is important to recognize that both operate along similar lines with their individual signifiers. In speaking of the reductive nature of human language, Devi exposes the fissures in it through a multivalent text of poetry that exploits this medium itself to undo its desire for stable definitions. Devi extends an invitation to the reader, which Ali accepts, to carry out a similar reading of her text. Both Devi and Ali are indulging in this interpretative drag that 'repeats [the referent] in order to remake [it]'. 'Drag', then, for a reader like Ali, means to write in constant awareness of Devi's poetic act. The self-conscious choices resulting from negotiations with 'voix' and 'langue' reveal the complex deliberation involved in creating the kind of postcolonial subject Devi is writing about

Postcolonial Perspectives, eds. A. McClintock, A. Mufti and E. Shohat, Minneapolis: University of Minnesota, 1997, pp. 381–95.

in French. If this identity is to remain in a mode of constant self-renewal, it cannot be a replication, or a simple reiteration. This identity, much like Devi's poetry collection, already recognizes Ali's presence as a reader, indeed as a listener, who is invested in Devi's conversation with the night.[3]

Mohit Chandna is an assistant professor in French and Francophone Studies at the English and Foreign Languages University in Hyderabad, India. He is the author of Spatial Boundaries, Abounding Spaces: Colonial Borders in French and Francophone Literature and Film *(Leuven University Press, 2021). Apart from EFLU, he has also taught at Cornell University and Jawaharlal Nehru University.*

---

3   Parts of this essay, or some ideas therein, have appeared in French in the following articles:

Mohit Chandna, 'Produire le non-lieu: l'Inde à la dérive chez Ananda Dévi', in *Caraivéti, Démarche de Sagesse: Numéro Spécial Sur Récit de Voyage*, ed. Gitanjali Singh, Delhi: Langers, July–December, 2017, pp. 63–67; Mohit Chandna, 'Femme et dislocation nationale chez Ananda Devi', in *Interculturel Francophonies*, Lecce: Alliance Française de Lecce, no. 28, 2015, pp. 119–33.

About the Author

Born in Mauritius, Ananda Devi has been writing for over four decades and is considered one of the major French language writers of Mauritius and the Indian Ocean. She is the author of twenty-four books of fiction, non-fiction and poetry. She has been awarded the Prix Radio France du Livre de L'Océan Indien for her novel *Moi, l'interdite,* the Prix des Cinq Continents de la Francophonie for her novel *Ève et ses décombres,* and the Prix Louis Guilloux for her novel *Le sari vert.* Her books *Pagli (Pagli), Eve de ses décombres (Eve Out of Her Ruins) Indian Tango (Indian Tango)* and *Les jours vivants (The Living Days)* have been translated into English. A native of Mauritius, Devi is considered to be one of the most important francophone writers in the world and was awarded the title of Chevalier des Arts et des Lettres by the French Government in 2010. In 2014, she received the Prix du Rayonnement de la langue et de la littérature françaises from the Académie Française.

About the Translator

Kazim Ali was born in the United Kingdom and has lived transnationally in the United States, Canada, India, France and the Middle East. His books encompass multiple genres, including several volumes of poetry, novels and translations, including books by Marguerite Duras, Sohrab Sepehri and Mahmoud Chokrollahi. He is currently a Professor of Literature at the University of California, San Diego. *All One's Blue: New and Selected Poems* is available from HarperCollins India. His newest books are a volume of three long poems entitled *The Voice of Sheila Chandra* and a memoir of his Canadian childhood, *Northern Light: Power, Land, and the Memory of Water*.

Thank you all
for your support.
We do this for you,
and could not do
it without you.

PARTNERS

pixel ||| texel

EMBREY FAMILY
FOUNDATION

ALLRED
CAPITAL MANAGEMENT
RAYMOND JAMES®

ADDITIONAL DONORS, CONT'D

Mark Haber
Mary Cline
Maynard Thomson
Michael Reklis
Mike Soto
Mokhtar Ramadan
Nikki & Dennis Gibson
Patrick Kukucka
Patrick Kutcher
Rev. Elizabeth & Neil Moseley
Richard Meyer

Scott & Katy Nimmons
Sherry Perry
Sydneyann Binion
Stephen Harding
Stephen Williamson
Susan Carp
Susan Ernst
Theater Jones
Tim Perttula
Tony Thomson

SUBSCRIBERS

Margaret Terwey
Ben Fountain
Gina Rios
Elena Rush
Courtney Sheedy
Caroline West
Brian Bell
Charles Dee Mitchell
Cullen Schaar
Harvey Hix
Jeff Lierly
Elizabeth Simpson

Nicole Yurcaba
Jennifer Owen
Melanie Nicholls
Alan Glazer
Michael Doss
Matt Bucher
Katarzyna Bartoszynska
Michael Binkley
Erin Kubatzky
Martin Piñol
Michael Lighty
Joseph Rebella

Jarratt Willis
Heustis Whiteside
Samuel Herrera
Heidi McElrath
Jeffrey Parker
Carolyn Surbaugh
Stephen Fuller
Kari Mah
Matt Ammon
Elif Ağanoğlu

AVAILABLE NOW FROM DEEP VELLUM

SHANE ANDERSON · *After the Oracle* · USA

MICHÈLE AUDIN · *One Hundred Twenty-One Days* · translated by Christiana Hills · FRANCE

BAE SUAH · *Recitation* · translated by Deborah Smith · SOUTH KOREA

MARIO BELLATIN · *Mrs. Murakami's Garden* · translated by Heather Cleary · *Beauty Salon* · translated by David Shook · MEXICO

EDUARDO BERTI · *The Imagined Land* · translated by Charlotte Coombe · ARGENTINA

CARMEN BOULLOSA · *Texas: The Great Theft* · *Before* · *Heavens on Earth* translated by Samantha Schnee · Peter Bush · Shelby Vincent · MEXICO

MAGDA CARNECI · *FEM* · translated by Sean Cotter · ROMANIA

LEILA S. CHUDORI · *Home* · translated by John H. McGlynn · INDONESIA

MATHILDE CLARK · *Lone Star* · translated by Martin Aitken · DENMARK

SARAH CLEAVE, ed. · *Banthology: Stories from Banned Nations* · IRAN, IRAQ, LIBYA, SOMALIA, SUDAN, SYRIA & YEMEN

LOGEN CURE · *Welcome to Midland: Poems* · USA

ANANDA DEVI · *Eve Out of Her Ruins* · translated by Jeffrey Zuckerman · MAURITIUS

PETER DIMOCK · *Daybook from Sheep Meadow* · USA

CLAUDIA ULLOA DONOSO · *Little Bird,* translated by Lily Meyer · PERU/NORWAY

RADNA FABIAS · *Habitus* · translated by David Colmer · CURAÇAO/NETHERLANDS

ROSS FARRAR · *Ross Sings Cheree & the Animated Dark: Poems* · USA

ALISA GANIEVA · *Bride and Groom* · *The Mountain and the Wall* translated by Carol Apollonio · RUSSIA

FERNANDA GARCIA LAU · *Out of the Cage* · translated by Will Vanderhyden · ARGENTINA

ANNE GARRÉTA · *Sphinx* · *Not One Day* · *In/concrete* · translated by Emma Ramadan · FRANCE

JÓN GNARR · *The Indian* · *The Pirate* · *The Outlaw* · translated by Lytton Smith · ICELAND

GOETHE · *The Golden Goblet: Selected Poems* · *Faust, Part One* translated by Zsuzsanna Ozsváth and Frederick Turner · GERMANY

SARA GOUDARZI · *The Almond in the Apricot* · USA

NOEMI JAFFE · *What are the Blind Men Dreaming?* · translated by Julia Sanches & Ellen Elias-Bursac · BRAZIL

CLAUDIA SALAZAR JIMÉNEZ · *Blood of the Dawn* · translated by Elizabeth Bryer · PERU

PERGENTINO JOSÉ · *Red Ants* · MEXICO

TAISIA KITAISKAIA · *The Nightgown & Other Poems* · USA

SONG LIN · *The Gleaner Song: Selected Poems* · translated by Dong Li · CHINA

JUNG YOUNG MOON · *Seven Samurai Swept Away in a River* · *Vaseline Buddha* translated by Yewon Jung · SOUTH KOREA

KIM YIDEUM · *Blood Sisters* · translated by Ji yoon Lee · SOUTH KOREA

JOSEFINE KLOUGART · *Of Darkness* · translated by Martin Aitken · DENMARK

YANICK LAHENS · *Moonbath* · translated by Emily Gogolak · HAITI

FORTHCOMING FROM DEEP VELLUM